NON-BEING AND NOTHINGNESS

Non-Being and Nothingness

THE NON-PHILOSOPHER
TIM SNAVELY

A Non-Prophet Organization

Contents

Chapter 1

To be, or not to be

The famous words of Shakespeare have permeated many cultures across the globe: *"To be, or not to be. That is the question."* This is the question that hits at the very core of existential angst if we indeed go about asking why our perceptions of existence require further explanation. Or we at least assume questions of continuing to be or not are central to an angsty being. The question does a nice job of reducing existence down to a pleasurable dichotomy of being and not being.

But what does it mean to be? And can we ever truly enter a mode of not being? Or rather, what exactly has ceased to be among those who choose or are otherwise forced into the state of *"not to be"?* To what extent are imaginary beings 'being'? And can we truly equivocate not being with Non-Being? I will let you be the judge as if I had any other choice in the matter. Unfortunately, we will not be able to trudge through these questions without referencing several different philosophical thinkers who have preceded me, nor will I be able to ignore a few circular presuppositions to reach any definitive existential conclusions (which will be made apparent in due time.)

So what exactly does it mean to be? To be is to currently be being. And to be being currently is to exist now, in time. These are built into the syntax of the language, at least for English. Martin Heidegger wrote a hefty and unnecessarily long book on this subject in German, but I'll cover him later. To make this obvious, and to expose the simplicity of the central theme behind *Being and Time*, let us like children ask what it means 'to jump,' which is a secondary mode of being that presupposes the being of the entity performing the jump, and the being of the object or subject being repelled. 'To jump' requires energy on the part of the entity performing the jump, right? And to jump can be said to mean to repel one's being off of a thing with enough energy to remove the being from the thing with some relative indication of vertical momentum.

Time is already riddled into the definition of the action, into the jump itself. When E = mc^2 is dimensionalized, it is mass multiplied by length squared divided by **time** squared. Therefore, it is impossible to jump off of anything, object or subject, without going through time.

And 'jump-ing' makes this time connection even more obvious, since a be-ing cannot be in the process of jump-ing without taking the time to be doing it. The suffix '-ing' connects the verb to a sequence of times for the action to happen, regardless if a thing was jumping, is jumping, will be jumping, or some combination of the three. Not only that, all verbs require and describe some mode of action, and action requires energy, and energy requires time. Only through the description of negation is the on-tological necessity for time averted to the verb, where the thing is not jumping or not being. And yet, even perpetual negation requires the possibility of a negation of the negation, in the sense of what is currently not jumping or not being, may at some point in time jump, or more fundamentally, come to be.

What is less obvious, however, is the definitional necessity for either mass or light in some form or combination for the action to take place in our shared observable reality. Even the actions contained in imaginary thought require the action of the brain or memory to maintain their effects on reality. The thinker adhering to the idea of solipsism would fight against mass's inclusion with space and time holding ontological priority in our Being if I'm not mistaken. This skepticism towards the being of other objects in the world likely stems from thinking similar to Renes Descartes' *Meditations*, where his famous climax is realized, his *"cogito sum"* otherwise stated as *"I think, therefore I am."*

Skepticism to an extreme degree of the reality of things being the way they are could and has been applied to the contents of what exactly this 'I' is made up of. Solipsism leads to the conclusion that the contents of 'I' do not extend beyond an active 'Null' consciousness in an otherwise empty abyss hallucinating or otherwise being tricked in the sense that our senses are completely wrong. It labels all other iterations that hold evidence for consciousness in the world as a scam; a set of mindless p-zombies and a projection of our own conscious-ness like a dream, and that Everything will cease to be as soon as 'I's' own consciousness taps out.

Luckily for you, my dear reader, this Super Null Hypothesis holds within itself the per-petual possibility of the negation of its own negation, since Everything can also be seen as evidence against this Super Null Hypothesis in the form of a negation of its own negation hav-ing already had happened in time, in the time al-ready past. And since we have already deduced that our conscious Being is contingent on time, as Being-in-active-thought, it then follows that solipsism is incorrect because ANY active con-sciousness MUST likewise exist IN TIME. So it is not just 'I,' and no more; the action of the thinking proves that there is SOMETHING beyond my consciousness and my Being, my am-ness, namely, time, and this time is almost certainly "not I."

I say 'almost certainly,' because in the case where 'I' houses the totality of time, and the totality of energy along with it, the proposition could still posit a certain kind of solipsism, even if it still doesn't negate the possibility of energy beyond the self. (I'll elaborate on this possibility later.)

But let's take this realization one step further, or rather, one step back to the (arguably) most useful thought Immanuel Kant brought to our current bank of knowledge. And that is that space is what he called an *'a priori'* concept, being alongside time as a thing that 'I am' innately aware of apart from experience. Time then exists outside of myself for the action of Being, the string of the 'I's' think-ing express-ing consciousness, and space then exists outside myself to contain and hold the set of things which are 'not-I' and distinguish them from 'I.'

I am being, therefore I am capable of action. Action requires space to distinguish action from inaction, even if that action is just my conscious awareness. So we currently have "I am being and thinking in space and time."

This may be circular, saying I am Being-in-Space-Time in one breath, then saying Space-Time-is-Being. This would suggest that Space-Time, likewise, requires action to validate their categorical existences as Primary Dimensions of energy in the world. One could posit that what was first discovered *'a posteriori,'* namely, dark energy's manifestation as the expansion of Space-Time, has now been deduced to be a thing consistent with reality *'a priori,'* as a fundamental action of the world where I am. Cool, I guess.

Space-Time-is-Being to hold the Being that is I who is thinking, therefore my thoughts are in action, AND Space-Time is in action. Maybe.

At this point, I question if mass or electromagnetism truly are necessary since vacuum energy perhaps could maintain an abysmal consciousness within a Space-Time that exists itself in its own meta-Space-Time, so that the Space-Time that is Being can Be-in-action. But in order for this meta-Space-Time to be included amongst the Beings that be, the meta-Space-Time must likewise be-in-action. This, in turn, would lead us to not just an infinite regression of First Causes, but First Spaces as well. (*Causality and time are either equivalent or indistinguishable when observed in isolation, because just as time is needed for causally-linked actions to occur, so does causality itself reveal how the actions are manifested in time.*)

Chapter 2

A Non-Being-
Space-Time-in-action

To break the infinite regression of First Space-Times, as well as to paradoxically continue it, we require Nothing to stop it. A Non-Being-Space-Time-in-action, as absurd as the notion sounds. So if we imagine Nothing, perfect absolute Nothingness, we can now count the set of things in this First-Space-Time that is Being. Clearly, there is not-a-single-thing Being, so there is not-a-single-thing to write down.

But wait a second! There is yet Nothing-Being, so we write down the one solitary Being in this perfect First-Space-Time: Nothing! This is the Non-Being at the crux of the paradox of existence, beyond which we can go no further...

But to go further still, the meta-Space-Time which contains the First Non-Being, we can be sure this particular meta-Space-Time is not being in any sense of the word because Nothing doesn't need to move to perform the action of splitting its singular and whole Non-Being. Nothing happened to the Non-existent Non-Being, because the whole Non-Being was and is, and will continue to be already split. (*If that sounds like nonsense, it was merely a sophist's way of saying 0/1=0/2. Keep that in mind as you continue reading.*)

So since the only necessary action needed to kick off Everything that is not Nothing can always be observed to have already happened, the First Non-Being, therefore, doesn't require its own meta-Space-Time, since the action in question can likewise be observed to have already happened within it. It does not matter if we ourselves are within the largest Space-Time only surrounded by the Non-Being, or within the smallest Space-Time within all other Space-Times that are also Being, we are all destined for Nothingness which represents this thing-in-itself philosophers apparently love talking about.

What I meant by "destined for Nothingness," is entropy increasing through time until all Beings that will ever come to be have ceased to be. Once all the Mass-Electric energy deteriorates via maximum dissipation into the far reaches of the perfect vacuum, time and space will shortly thereafter cease to have any intelligible meaning to their Being, since their meaning of Being are construed and made relative to the other objects within their Being.

Once all the things that can be or otherwise be self-aware have become Non-existent, Space-Time's Being will also cease their Being to make way and transition into a state of Non-Being. Or rather, become the next otherwise empty meta-Space-Time to be the next Non-Being that will be immobile to do anything, save for appearing to be split as well. The First Non-Being cannot think about its own Non-Being, since it is not within its own meta-Space-Time to perform active thoughts. But hypothetically, Non-First-Non-Beings could subsequently "think" (at least it does not contradict). These subsequent Non-Beings would, like a traditional solipsist, be aware of what was going on within Themselves, since They would be free to think within their own meta-Space-Time that endured after the last set of Everything perished. It would work just as well if these Non-Beings lacked self-awareness like the First Non-Being, simply Being-inside-the-dead-carcasses-of-Space-Times-past, or as Heidegger may have put it, Being in a Space-Time that is merely present-at-hand, but no longer ready-to-hand for anything, but I should digress away from these Non-falsifiable statements that have no bearing on our current state of Being.

But I should say, that although mass and electromagnetism do not bear any ontological necessity for the 'I's' thinking consciousness since vacuum energy could instigate the actions necessary for a simulated conscious awareness, our current state of consciousness Being-a-Non-Non-Being, and Beings that represent a negation of the negation, do vehemently necessitate the Mass-Electric existentially to keep... you know... existing. So a testament for us to collectively be a sincere negation of the negation is your continued awareness during my sleep, and while I'm still alive, my awareness during yours. If you are reading this after I die, then congratulations! Our existence is sincere... well, not mine anymore in your time in the future... (Zilch damn it!), but yours certainly is, seeing that the quality of your thoughts is now, in my future, sharing in the thoughts of a dead man.

(But Tim, it could still be an illusion of my own making. It could still be a false negation, and Nothing has been negated beyond your belief in a sincere negation!)

Listen here, you hypothetical solipsist... either Nothing is real, or Nothing is really and sincerely negated at the moment, and seeing that you are now thinking in action, either YOU are a Non-Being and a God holding within yourself the totality of energy, or YOU in your Being conquered God in your active negation of Their negation. You can go your own way!

YOU decide which is better! Will the will of Nil be fulfilled in you? Zilch no! Not if I, the Non-Prophet and the Non-Philosopher, can help it! Don't lose yourself in thinking you are all that exists, my dear Null. You NEED space and time to think. You are not, no, you are incapable of being Nobody; the Nothing Whole, exactly because you are capable of thought! So humble yourselves, because God is dead, and you are not dead, therefore, live in both pride and horror at your successful negation of the Great Negation in the sky!

This brings to mind another flaw of presupposing an infinite god of somethingness (I.G.O.S.) in the place of the Non-Being also named here as Nobody. In many theist traditions, God is claimed to be simultaneously omnipresent and eternal as well as being spaceless and timeless, or otherwise BEYOND Space-Time. We have already deduced how a thinking Being requires Space & Time to be in active thought. So if an I.G.O.S is Being, the demonstrability of its thoughts should be represented within the finitude of all else that is Being.

(But Tim, His thoughts are higher than your thoughts! His ways are higher than your ways!)

Ah! But here is the thing, you hypothetical

theist: we can represent the thoughts of the infinite God with math equations or word structures. They could be replicated like this, and in fact, is it not you who claim to know the true words of God and the words and actions that are pleasing or unpleasant to Him? Are not the words of God a reflection of His thoughts?

Am I God to you, that my thoughts are higher than yours for noticing that higher thoughts need to be communicated to distinguish the higher thoughts from a complete lack of thought? No, of course not. A true I.G.O.S. can use His Big-Boy words just like the rest of us. Albert Einstein's thoughts and many others like him have had thoughts that are higher than ours, yet they still require communication in some form to demonstrate any thought at all.

The abstractions derived from infinities are possible, so it would be most beneficial to write them down. It is rather sad actually, seeing that the current equations for God are no better than "You + Me = Love" and "You - Me = Hate" which... hang on a minute... I know this is a strawman equation, but let's steelman it up a bit and actually see where it goes....

(DISCLAIMER! The end of this chapter ends up going Nowhere! You can either skip to chapter 3 if you want more finger-licking-good ontology or finish this chapter for the laughs and the raised eyebrows.)

The Bible says God is love, and that I fall short of His glory to inherently go to heaven, otherwise, this shortcoming leads to either hell or something hell-like that merely stands for being separated from God.

If [God=Love], then [Love-God=0], [God-Love=0], [Love/God=1], & [God/Love=1]. If I am less than God, [I<Love], & [I<God]. This shortcoming is a difference, which is a fancy way of saying subtraction, so [I-God=Hell]. It then follows that [I=Hell+God], [Hell+God-I=0], & [I-Hell-God=0]. *Hell must also be some negative number if it is the result of the difference between a greater thing from a lesser thing.*

This is all fine, so far. I think the equations thus far hold no contradictions with what the Bible proposes. Heaven, if it was to be in a similar equation, could either be an additive or a multiplicative function. Either we must add the gift of God's mercy to 'I's' being, or His blessings cause fruitful multiplication which climax with multiplying with God Himself as a part of the Bride of Christ (the church). [(I+God)] can stand for the multiplicative identity of 1, then leave the variable x to allow God to determine how and when to bring extra positivity (blessings) to your life and afterlife. So, [(I+God)x=Heaven(later) and blessings(now)]. Now we can simply solve for x.

Almost immediately, we can see that different numbers for x provide interesting and contradictory solutions. When x is a negative number, like in the instance of Job in the Bible, we see God being the cause of Job's curses. When x is 0, no change happens, and Heaven and the benefits of God become Non-existent. Heaven can be anything we want it to be with God, by the looks of it.

But let's assume the baseline, when $x=1$, and the equation for salvation and the blessings of God are as simple as [I+God=Heaven], which is a standard gospel message. Just believe in God, receive Jesus, and Heaven's Gate is certain for you to see one day. Add God to yourself, and you will be saved. If [I+God=Heaven], then

[I=Heaven-God], [Heaven-God-I=0], & [I+God-Heaven=0].

*Here is where the real madness begins...*Given all the assumptions above, which again, are consistent with Biblical proposals, [I-Hell-God=I+God-Heaven], the 'I's' cancel out, and the 2 God's can combine, and the negative Hell and Heaven and be added to both sides to make the TRUTH of Christianity say...[2God+Hell=Heaven]. 2 God's in Hell is Heaven. Seems legit.

I then plugged these equations into WolframAlpha, to see if the TRUTH of Christianity can tell us the answer to "What am I?" The answer is hilarious, to me at least. When I am a Christian, and when God is not a Non-Being or a -1-Being, I am equal to -2God(God-1)/God+1. In other words, when [God=g, and $g \neq 0$ *or* -1, I=-2g(g-1)/g+1]

Several things come to my attention, which I will briefly bring to yours as well. The only values for a positive God that end with I being positive occur between 0 and 1. Beyond 1, the greater the number attributed to God, the more negative the self becomes. The greatest and most positive self in the kingdom of heaven is one who puts God's number around 0.4142, which provides the output of their own number around 0.3431.

Hell also has an interesting solution of note, under the same premises for g. [$g{\neq}0$ or -1, Hell=g-$3g^2$/g+1]. The only thing of significant interest to note, for the Christian, is that the value for Hell is positive when the value of God is between 0 & 0.333. That, and it's funny to me that it is impossible to define Hell without God, even when Hell is usually defined by the absence of God. (The Christian cannot get rid of God, even in Hell, apparently, which is actually consistent with His omnipresence.)

But remember what I said earlier? The value for Hell *must* be negative, as the difference between 'I' and God. And the only values of God which lead to a negative Hell fall between -1-0, and 0.333-infinity. So at least we figured out that God is most likely not a negative number value, to the Christian, but it doesn't negate the possibility entirely.

Heaven is then when [$g{\neq}0$ or -1, Heaven=$2g$+(g-$3g^2$/g+1)]. Ultimately, it doesn't matter, since *g* cannot be pinned down to any function or value in itself, other than the value ranges expressed in the previous paragraph. *For God being claimed to be a Solid Rock, He sure seems to be being-a-Variable.* And even though Christianity's equations would like to suggest that God cannot be Nothing, plugging 0 into all three of those equations for *g* doesn't actually break any laws of math. If God is 0, then Heaven is 0, Hell is 0, and I am 0. Then all that truly remains beyond the Christian framework is 'I' figuring out what exactly '0' means.

Chapter 3

Being is being, but a being isn't Being

But I've done enough here. It's not my job to figure out the logic or the lack thereof behind other people's theology for them. The ONLY way I can comprehend these ludicrous equations being dismissible from the git-go is by performing a dimensional analysis on the separate things in question, which you could then quickly see that I equated places with the things inside the places, which obviously isn't true in its totality. A place can be defined by the total sum of things contained within the space that also defines the place, but those individual things within the place are not the place, if those things can be removed from the place without losing any meaning concerning where the place is.

Even the arguably more valid equation of God = Love falls apart for equating the substantive noun in question with the verb attributed to the noun. It's a common confusion, no doubt, but a confusion nonetheless. For example, although we would be correct to say that "there is a being that is being," it would be erroneous to leave out the few words that would make the statement "a being is being." Not because it can be understood the same way, but because it can more readily show us how even the correct saying can be used to equivocate incorrectly. Not because the actions of being implies a being that is being, but because the word 'is' is a linking verb that can imply both the connection of the noun to the verb, and equivalence of what is before to what is after the word 'is.' Zilch is Nada is Nothing is Zero; equivocating nouns to their synonymous nouns is fine. Connecting nouns to their appropriate definitions is also fine. Even actively negating certain connections by saying what the thing is not is fine, even if it doesn't get us any closer to what it is.

Since words in and of themselves don't hold any inherent meaning outside of their cultural and language contexts, creating meaningful connections from the word to the culture at large is necessary to form an intelligible understanding of what is being communicated. But 'being is being' is either wrong or a tautology that gets us Nowhere: The verb of being is the verb of being, and the noun who is a being is that form of a noun which is being. A being is not Being, because a being doesn't hold within itself the totality of that which is Being, but only a fragment. And a being is not necessarily being, simply because the possibility of the negating position of the thing, as a thing being inactive or being unmoved can still be attributed to a being without negating the Being underlying it. However, Being is always being, because the actions consistent with being implies the movement of the Being-thing in action. And when the lack of action is applied to Being in its totality, this is precisely what it means to be Non-Being. *I just distinguished being (v) from being (n-general) from Being (n-specific ontological basis), in case you're confused...*

Now, if you are as unconvinced of this as I am (mainly for its absurdity); perhaps we are now both ready for the circular silliness of distinguishing Being from Non-Being more clearly. As beings who think, or at least who are alive and aware, we have never seen a non-being state of action *in its totality*. We have only ever seen being unmoved for itself. Total Non-Being, by definition, could not be observed by Beings. So we are left with one solitary thing that is Not-Being-in-any-form, which is the thing of Non-Being, which is Nothing in its totality.

This leaves us with literally Everything being what is Being, which again, gets us Nowhere closer to defining what it is. Earlier in this book, we used pure reason to conclude "I am a Being in active thought within a Space-Time." And yet, we have no way of determining the pureness of this reasoning, nor are we capable of creating an actualized example of a Non-Being to contrast against this 'I' who is Being!

And since Everything that is not Non-Being is Being, am I, therefore, Everything?! Or at least Everything except for the Space-Time that holds 'I'? The indeterminate certainty from this question stems from the same indeterminate certainty of the mass and electromagnetic dimensions' ontological necessity towards our Being since it is only from those dimensions that any hint of quantity in the appearance of the multiplicity of beings emerges.

So by reason alone, since there is no reason to conclude that any reasoning is pure, by whatever means we come to these conclusions, what conclusions at least appear to be the most universal? In a single sentence, this is Everything beyond Nothing that we can know for certain: I am an actively thinking Being within at least a 2-Dimensional Space-Time.

Aha! Eureka! A certainty of multiplicity! There are, at minimum, 3 things that need to be Being: I, space, & time!

What an interesting thought! I may be, with a non-zero degree of likelihood, an active 0-D point moving freely through a line of space through a line of time. I continue further, for beyond the space & time outside 'I,' there should yet be a metaphysical indicator of sorts, either beyond 'I' or within 'I,' to determine what exactly the different values of space at different times will mean once I pass through them. May I myself, space itself, or time itself be the attributor of space's units of value? If it is I, I would need to then be ahead of myself in determining what the values of the units of space would mean in the future. Either this or the I who thinks now is 'Now' is actually lagging behind the other I in the past, while this other I is in the true 'Now.' *(It's this second one, in actuality...)*

As for space, can its Being determine its own values of meaning? Perhaps, but it would require an additional degree of freedom to do so. There may be, in that particular Space-Being's case, another Being attributing space's attribution of its own values deterministically. There may be an infinite regression of first deceivers as such if Everything we observe in common is a deception.

But the deduction (bare minimum), is that there is at least one other form of a Being-thing that attributes meaning to units of space in order for such an initial deception to take place. Whether it be the case that there are 2 'I's' with 1 deceiving the other, or another being in Space-Time, space in itself in a 2-D space of self-being, time in itself in a 2-D self-causing self-being, math itself overlaying values beforehand, or another active being actively deceiving me within its own meta-Space-Time, we and I may never know.

This arbiter of values in space need not be in active thought to play their part as a deceiver of reality, but merely be an additional stagnant dictation that determines how the deception is simulated. Like, for example, programming in a computer game made by a now-dead creator who determined which inputs are required to attain certain outputs within the game. Again, if a 2-D Space-Time can be in action in relation to itself, to be ever-expanding, this action can, in turn, be translated into active thoughts in relation to itself. If this translation of action into thought remains possible, I then find myself asking yet another question: is it possible for 'I' to be Space-Time itself misattributing my own actions as my thoughts?

Yes! It's possible, then, to be my own

deceiver in this case, where I am simply Space-Time (or even a set fragment of Space-Time) in action, misattributing my actions as thoughts conceived with the meaning that I attributed to it after the actions took place! Clever girl, I am, tricking myself in such a convincing manner! Or is it "clever boy?" I don't even know anymore! I guess it is possible that I just don't know what I'm observing until it is observed, then I give the actions meaning after they already happened. No other arbiter of values is needed.

So the certainty of multiplicity disappears, under the guise of the statement: I may be Being as Space-Time in action in itself.

To all of philosophy's horror, if anyone is to follow this absurdly plausible axiom to various conclusions, René Descartes could be reasonably refuted concerning his "*cogito sum*," since the actions underlying the thoughts would be what underlies the certainty of my Being. So it is now "**I act, therefore I am**," not, "*I think, therefore I am*." Absolute absurdity; there may yet be no thought to be had, but an endless misattribution of actions as thought!

Chapter 4

What follows from "I am not the totality."

What else is there to meditate on? Being's meaning can be summarized by the totality of actions performed. Non-Being is the totality of inaction. Shakespeare's 'not-to-be' is the yearning to cease action whilst still in action, as a possible negation of the negation of the Negation.

Shall we trudge through the venture of the state of Being for imaginary beings? Yes, we shall, for active thought may yet be revived with certainty, or maybe not. In the mildly silly self-deceiver "I am merely an active Space-Time" scenario, Nothing significantly changes, it just goes 1 level deeper. Just as I could misattribute my actions as thoughts, so too could I attribute these thoughts with phantom actions that were never performed in the first place.

I could say, "Oh, I could have acted in that way at that time; I shall now correct my error!" But the act of acting that way at that time shall never change, since that time has passed, that much is certain. But the very actions of reflecting on your thoughts are only ever being in active thought, which again, is at least possibly, a misattribution of our actions. You may even imagine an imaginary being having thoughts of their own; it doesn't matter! They, as in all imaginary thoughts, can be placed right alongside real objective things as misattributions of your actions. This reasoning is precisely why it is better to presuppose that 'I am not Space-Time-in-itself-and-by-itself,' because if it isn't supposed at all, solipsism would strike back hard, and there would be no meaningful distinction between the actions driving imagined beings and the actions driving Being in the real world.

So even while we grant the aforementioned possibility of misattributing actions as thought, we can better distinguish the inner world of thought, reason, imagination, and subject from the outer world of our objectively shared reality comprised of energy if we don't. So instead I'd rather err on the side of the more reasonable presupposition, that 'the totality of energy underlying all that is observed to be being is genuine,' which implies that my entity within Mass-Electric-Space-Time is reasonably close to as it appears, due to the entity's dependence on this same genuine energy.

With only those 2 presuppositions acknowledged and shared, our collective *a posteriori* knowledge found in the scientific method can again make reasonable sense, and help distinguish our being in action that affects the objective world, with our being in active thought that only affects our inner subjective world (even if those thoughts often later motivate us towards certain actions).

So let's ask again: with those 2 reasonable presuppositions of energy genuinely underlying that which appears to be being, and I am not the totality of this energy, what is the nature of Being for imaginary beings? This provides us with a more reasonable answer! The extent of their Being is contingent on our neural network's ability to create or otherwise comprehend their character Being-in-the-world. Our understanding; our contemplations are the extent that these imaginary beings are Being-in-the-world-alongside-us-in-human-reality. Beyond this, they are being-in-the-art; existing in their worlds, as the pictures, sounds, textures, and other sensory phenomena attributed to them by our inner subjects.

But beyond THAT, Nothing is connecting these imaginary beings to our shared *"human-reality,"* as Jean-Paul Sartre would say. We are the ones who bring these mere ideas into Being-in-the-world-alongside-us-in-human-reality. We are the ones who will choose and have chosen which imaginary beings are worthy of being replicated in the neural networks of our culture at large. We are the ones who act on their behalf since they are incapable of any sort of being or action without us. Our actions are what bring imaginary beings into Being.

For religion, our actions are what bring our fictitious beliefs to life, even if it would be better if they remained dead. For politics, our actions are what turn our common disgruntled opinions into either reform or revolution, even if such actions may accelerate us to a state of being dead. For science, likewise, our reasonably held true beliefs backed by replicable methodologies can only be brought into being by our actions. If the extraneous actions are minimal for seekers of the truth, as is common for adherers to world peace, then the over-the-top actions of liars and charlatans will snuff out the efficacy of the truth. Like magicians, they are masters of misdirection.

Pardon my own tangential misdirection, but why do you think comedians are so successful, hmmm? They start with a baseline expectation, be it a story, observation, joke format, or form of presentation, THEN THEY HIT YOU WITH THE PUNCHLINE holding the unexpected truth hidden within the scenario. Comedians lead you with a carrot, then HIT YOU WITH THE

STICK OF TRUTH. Mystery as an imaginary genre does this as well. The mystery is about finding the unknown within the constraints of the imaginary novel. Sometimes the Stick of Truth hurts, like, "Sorry Billy, it was your father who killed your mother by stabbing her 40 times in the chest after finding out that she was once a man and kept that info from him. Yes, that's right Billy, you were also adopted. And your real father is R Kelly." The truth may hurt, but you don't necessarily have to make it sting to get the desired effect of getting people to listen to it. So naturally, we can make the truth prevail by hitting people with sticks until they understand it, performing relevant science experiments to prove the truth, or simply being more interesting than the quacks who don't actually know the truth by amusingly debunking them.

Chapter 5

Quantum Bits don't bite unless you ask

So let's Segway into the nature of the truth about Non-Being. I have said it in the past, and I'll say it again here as a condensed reformulation of Snavely's Conundrum. There is a true claim that X exists. If X exists, then it is within the set of Everything that exists. If "the set of Everything that exists" exists, then it should be the case that it both contains itself and paradoxically includes and excludes Nothing-that-does-not-exist.

Now originally, I made it follow that Nothing then must be the First Cause to essentially cause the First Thing that would be within Everything that exists. Since it is logically in-coherent for a thing to cause itself to be, and because the Non-Being is not being, how could the Non-Being split into its Non-Being and Being-Nothing states to kickstart Everything that exists in the first place?

This solution, that the Non-Being is already split to begin with led me to ask the question if the Non-Being that is currently Being-Nothing is also capable of demonstrating that it is like-wise already split or not. *(I know, it's a silly ques-tion, but bear with me.)* If the photon's energy is spaceless, timeless, and immaterial and can be split inherently with an immediately replicable single-slit interference pattern, in the fullness of its Being, what does this imply for Nothing's Being?

Perhaps a better question is "what meaning-fully distinguishes a photon from Nothing?" Vacuum energy versus light energy. The 0 0-D point, versus the 1 0-D point. Nobody versus the infinitesimal representation of I.G.O.S. ful-filling Her, (to those aware of *The Gospel of Zilch & Nada.*) Nothing as Nothing versus Nothing as Something. It appears the light itself is all that distinguishes endarkenment from enlightenment. Literally and figuratively.

So what if, *now hear me out*, our universe is contained within a photon? And other photons within the simple electromagnetic wave function are the contents of our multiverse within another universe, and photons hold in them "the set of Everything that exists" within them as well? There is not much else to the photon that is objectively meaningful beyond its wave function and its approximate energetic particle form, after all. Only a Non-Being could reasonably stop this infinite regress of first photon-like containers of non-negatable world energy.

So with this line of thinking, our photon; our I.G.O.S., as the Non-Being's first Being, would likely be a single, solitary point of light energy. It is energy suspended in Nowhere, being in itself spaceless, timeless, without mass, *(which would make it merely traditional $E=mc^2$ energy, otherwise)*, in a perpetual superposition of states between Being-in-action, given the number 1, and Non-Being, given the number 0. In this superposition, it would be acting, (as in,

Being-in-active-thought) as a single-bit quantum computer simulating the set of Everything that exists. That is if light could meaningfully exist by itself like that.

Simulation Theory couldn't compete with Photon Theory, for every simulation in Simulation Theory would emit even more photons to simulate Everything naturally! Muahaha!

Welp, that's enough writing for today. There is a fine line between brilliance and crazy, and I may have crossed the line into Crazy Town. Meta-Crazy-Town, since, you know, I am working in a mental health hospital. But the brilliance can be summed up with this short TL;DR: It *is* simulation theory, but the "matrix" is a single quantum bit of light energy in superposition.

But naturally, as I do, more questions popped up in my mind concerning the Quantum Light Bit. If we are within a QLB, how is space still actively expanding? Could it be that Everything is simply constantly-shrinking-to-make-Space-Time-appear-to-be-in-active-expansion-in-human-reality? It could, but we've already chosen to suppose that the energy underlying Being is genuine. Or could the Cosmic Microwave Back-ground be the QLB barrier? Mayhaps, but there is no way to tell.

And couldn't a Quantum Vacuum Bit be just as likely and stable to be the First Being? Absolutely, because from both, all beings from such a Non-Being could emerge; and it can be observed that vacuum energy & light energy are within the set of Everything that exists.

That's not the problem. The problem is, I say in writing again, that the paradoxically uni-fied answer to the question of *"why is there something rather than nothing?,"* is in the ques-tion's simultaneous negation and affirmation in stating that "Nothing is a possible state of Being." Maybe it is not "absolutely Nothing cannot be observed," but rather "because abso-lutely Nothing cannot be observed to contrast against something, how can we be sure that what we are observing isn't Nothing?" We can doubt and be uncertain in Everything, yes, even the essence of our Being, seeing that all action could have started from a definitionally INAC-TIVE (within its meta-Space-Time) QLB or QVB. Wouldn't this make the opposing Non-sensical question of "why is there Nothing rather than something?" become just as valid of a question in this case, if the "something" has likewise not been observed in itself?

The dichotomous Bits are my examples of Being-as-Non-Being, as a First Cause. In the case of the QVB, it is not just Nothing, as a Non-Being, but it is also infinitesimally Something that paradoxically negates its very negating property of itself by its Being-whilst-inactive. It shouldn't be able to do this, it would be the totality of Non-sense if it existed whilst performing no actions to distinguish itself to be included amongst the set of Everything that is Being. But because the Non-Being has already been split, we can see how the negation of perpetually absolute Non-Being was and is and will be successful in our very Being.

Let me explain. By doubting the Non-Being's success, we continue either in our indeterminate state of Being, (which is exactly as both the QLB and the QVB already are) or continue in Wrong Understanding of our Being as Being-Absolute-in-some-form, as Descartes and solipsists did. By affirming its success, we both validate the Non-Being's Being-whilst-inactive, and we also validate Nothing by stating that Nothing is.

Chapter 6

It is what its
is-ness is

Is the equivocation of 'being' and 'is' a true or false one? Probably a false one, because as stated earlier, 'being' implies an action in some form in time, but 'is' does not carry with it such an implication. But, much like how being implies the Being of a being, so does 'is' implies the is-ness of that which it is. When it is what it is, its is-ness is it, and it is Nobody's and Everybody's business to question what the is-ness of it is.

The investigation of possible negation is what gives is-ness its power. What or who is it?

Where is it? How is it that way? Why is it that way? Thus, since 'is' is not constrained to be physical in-the-world, is-ness can equivocate what it is mathematically and qualitatively as well, and hold true even whilst being inactive in and of itself, bypassing the question of its objective state of Being.

What 'is' is, is equivocating whatever the subject making the statement puts before and after the 'is'. What 'is-ness' is, is the totality of what a subject could potentially reasonably and truly equivocate to 'it'. It (the before) is (the equivocation of) what it is (the after, which is its is-ness). And since 'what it is' is its is-ness, it *is* its is-ness! So if it is an object, its is-ness can be broken down into its objective and subjective qualities. If it is a subjective thing, or if we acknowledge that only the object's subjective qualities are up for discussion, what it is is up for debate; its is-ness is up for debate.

Even when we say "this is what makes up the object," the objectification of the object is oftentimes incomplete, and can likewise be debated. For example, when does a cup become a bowl, or when does a cup become a non-cup, and become something else like a jug, mug, or plate? Are shot glasses cups? Is what makes up a cup existentially connected to its equipmentality to be used and be ready-to-hand as a cup-like object in the world of concern?

Perhaps. *"It is a cup, until it is not a cup!"* cries a subject. "Ah! But its cup-ness is an abstraction of your perceptions perceiving it to be used as an equipment of Being-a-cup!" cries the Negator! *"Yeah, so?"* inquires a subject. The Negator answers, "If a cup is merely your perception of it Being-a-cup; if it is how I, my subject, sees what it is, then even the is-ness of the object Being-a-cup is up for a reasonable subject's debate to demonstrate that the object-in-question is NOT Being-a-cup.

"I am what I am." declared a subject. "Ah! But your am-ness, being merely the 1st-person singular form of is-ness, is likewise the abstraction of your perceptions perceiving yourself to being your own equipment, as Being-yourself! Tell me, my dear subject, what is the self's am-ness while you're not perceiving yourself Being-yourself?" The subject proposes, *"My am-ness would continue as Being-schizophrenic."* The Negator

tries once more, "Ah! But what is the self's am-ness while you're not perceiving yourself as Being-yourself, nor as Being-schizophrenic?" The subject, who may as well be me, gives a final rebuttal, "My am-ness would continue as Being-an-idiot-in-my-own-world-alongside-Nobody-in-active-imagination-whilst-actively-negating-myself-to-the-point-of-Being-like-the-Non-Being-which-indeterminately-Be's-as-Its-Primary-Mode-of-Being-in-the-world-alongside-us-in-human-reality-Zilch-damn-it-I-am-hungry-I-can-go-for-some-tacos-Being-alongside-and-inside-myself-in-human-reality-right-now-*Splat*-AWW-Shit-Got-Frank's-Hot-sauce-on-the-page-because-I-put-that-shit-on-the-set-of-Everything-that-exists-hashtag-not-sponsored-but-hashtag-would-love-to-be-sponsored-because-I-believe-Frank's-is-Being-a-badass-hot-sauce-in-the-world-alongside-us-in-human-reality-and-I-hope-they-continue-to-Be-a-badass-forever-more-Ramen." But enough about this am-ness, that only has applications to the self.

Chapter 7

The Brotherhood of Chairs

There is more to say concerning is-ness! And we shall investigate the depths of is-ness by asking the most mundane of questions and asking 'What is it?' and 'What is it not?'

For example, what is a chair? What is not a chair? And is there any defining feature that can be given to a chair that cannot hold true for any other household object? What about the chair's capability to be used as equipment?

Let's talk about the features of the chair first, since it will tell us its dimensions. A stereotypical chair has 3 key features: a seat (with the primary function being to sit an object on), a back (with its function to help the sitter remain sitting), and legs (with the function to elevate the seat above the plane of the floor). Some chairs have arms to aid the back with its function. Some chairs have belts or tables adhered to them for added safety and utility. But the stereotypical chair has legs, a back, and a seat.

Here we shall ask if there are any of the components of a chair necessary to keep its usefulness as a word describing a thing Being-in-the-world-alongside-us-in-human-reality? Well, backs aren't necessary, since there are some saddle chairs named as such with just its seat, and some stools are likewise functional chairs as well. And the legs aren't really necessary either, since stadium chairs are legless within the stadium context, and barber-shop chairs function with only 1 leg.

At first glance, only something needs to be in place to make the seat not on the floor to make it a chair. But does a stadium chair become not a chair when it is removed from the stadium context? Can a stadium chair lay bare in the meadow and lose its Title of Chairhood? Maybe, there surely is an argument to be had there. But if the stadium chair doesn't lose its Chairhood in a meadow, can just the seat of the stool maintain any hope of maintaining its Title of Chairhood? Even less so.

The question now becomes, in light of this ambiguous disk in a meadow being a chair or not, is seat-ness required within a chair's is-ness? Does the seat MAKE the chair? If we absurdly remove the seat, but return the legs, back, and arms into their proper place, and ask a sitter to rest their weight on the chair-in-question's arms and back, is it good enough to say that this object has joined the Brotherhood of Chairs? Perhaps it would, either as the arms becoming the seat of the chair, or as the object sim-ply Being-a-broken-or-incomplete-chair-that-people-kept-procrastinating-on-replacing-the-seat. If it isn't a chair, then no part is inherently necessary to the chair's is-ness, if we likewise negate its back and legs as being-necessary to a chair.

If the warped-and-uncomfortable-and-diffi-cult-to-sit-on-chair is a chair, which it surely is, then it would be wrong to bar Vlad the Impalers impaling poles from the beloved Brotherhood of Chairs as well.

And me! I'm a chair! You're a chair! Everything is a chair! Is Nothing a chair, or is Everything a chair? Or are there only things that are more chair-like than others, even when there is only the Non-chair in the middle of the Being-a-chair abstraction? *(This is the way I see it.)*

As equipment, a thing is more chair-like if it functions well as a seat. Then it is more chair-like if its seat feature is off the ground. A chair is more chair-like when it aids the sitter-in-question in sitting upright, relative to the ground. A chair for me may be a bed for a guinea pig. A chair becomes less chair-like as it is elongated to fit multiple people, and becomes more bench-like or couch-like. A chair becomes less chair-like when the seating plane is jaggedly sharp or otherwise unfit or unsafe for sitting on, like a chair of nails or an impaling pole.

Now don't get me wrong, we can still define the dimensional features of a particular chair-like object. And we can define it according to its function as equipment, like how we can observe what Merriam-Webster did when they defined a chair as:

1. *a seat* typically having four legs and a back *for one person*
2. *an official seat* or *a seat* of authority, state, or dignity.
3. a position of employment usually of one occupying a chair desk
4. *Any various devices that hold up or support.*

But although the particular chair-like object is objective in nature, made of Mass-Electric 'stuff,' the chair-ness of the chair is subjective and relative to the object capable of sitting in the chair. Tiny chairs are for dolls to sit on, and giant chairs are for mythically proportionate imaginary giants to sit on (or for people with equally mythically gigantic egos who think the chair is fitting for them).

But the chair's is-ness is not, in all likelihood, because it adds Nothing to the chair-ness of the chair. And the last time I checked, 0 necessary parts for a chair + 0 necessary atoms for a chair + 0 necessary subjects to use a chair as equipment + 0 necessary attributes for a chair = 0 chairs to be observed. The chair is Non-Being.

But this chair, this particular chair that is being sat in by my plumpish ass, this cube-ish chair that exclusively refracts blue electro-magnetic waves as perceived by my retinas, maintains a mass of about 15 pounds, a back that reaches ~36 inches off the ground, arms that solidly protrude ~27 inches off the ground, and a seat ~18 inches off the ground, with 4 thick legs whose precise dimensional analysis would be too long to describe, is Being-in-the-world-alongside-me-right-now-in-time-in-human-reality.

Chapter 8

The post-postmodernists finally lost the Vogue-ness!

As an intriguing but related tangent, Vogue-ness is a form of Being, didn't you know? It is essentially Being-with-whatever-is-cool-in-the-moment. The Vogue-ness of society is precisely what is discarded in the postmodern movement. To go beyond the modern, you have to become postmodern. An unspecified shift from whatever is Being-cool-right-now towards Being-whatever-the-self-thinks-will-be-cool-in-the-future.

But, as it stands, whatever is not cool is still a form of Being, it's just Being-lame. And ironically, if postmodernism caught on amongst the populace at the moment and ceased Being-lame, then it would just become modernism again.

So to get ahead, and stay ahead, the post-postmodernists arose seemingly out of No-where to ensure that they stayed ahead of the modern, always living in the future, but never now. But unfortunately, upon the release of the movie, *Honey, We Shrunk Ourselves*, the post-postmodernists were perturbed to discover that *"The Future....is NOW!,"* which made their precious ideology succumb to the hungry modernist Vogue once again.

The same fate met the post-post-postmodernists and the post-post-post-postmodernists... they got way too popular and fell from their highly intricate ideologies stacked like an endless tower of Post-it Notes.

Then, on one fateful day, a single post-post-post-post-postmodernist discovered nihilism.

They found the truth that was eating at the base of their ideology, and that was the fact that "Nothing can escape from the Vogue!" So the postmodernist way of thinking could finally be free from the wretched plebs of filthy modern thinking.

They found the ultimate form of postmodernism, and ZILCH DAMN IT, IT IS GETTING TOO COOL TO BE A NIHILIST TOO!

So what, then, can be safe from the Vogue? Pre-modernist thought, perhaps? Shall critical thought eternally regress to the point of minimal or no thought in the name of anti-Vogueness?

Yes. And that is why postmodernist thinking suddenly got really quiet. *The Vogue got to them*...Therefore, the thoughts held in the head of the modern postmodernist are in a state of Non-Being. *It was the only way to lose the Vogue!*

This is relevant because we can use this Non-modernist realization to investigate is-ness more thoroughly. We can ask, for a chair that is Vogue, does the Vogue-ness add anything to the chair's is-ness? The answer, rather than being a certain "no," is more of a "to what degree?" or more like "depends on who is investigating the is-ness of the chair."

The reasoning for this, if the reasoning was attempted to be demonstrated, is that if you indirectly ask what a thing, or more specifically, a chair-in-itself is, we have concluded that there is Nothing there since No-single-thing can be in itself without having 2 selves. However, when we go about indirectly asking what qualities a thing has, this bypasses the 2-self requirement for asking what a thing is in itself and instead asking what a thing is itself.

Even if the precise level of Vogue-ness a thing has can vary from person to person, asking what level of Vogue-ness a particular chair has will always be a valid question to ask! The answer will likewise be a valid answer, even if the Vogue units used to reach a particular value are unknown and unstandardized. All things under investigation, even an apparent absence of things can be asked how Vogue this particular thing-of-appearance is. So even when there is Nothing at the core of the thing-in-itself, the set of potential qualities that can be used to describe the is-ness of the thing are not Null and adds understanding to what the thing is when a common understanding is held concerning what such a quality means when it is attributed to a thing.

Chapter 9

Yes, No, 4 rocks, and None of the Above

Let's now return to I's 'am-ness,' now that the displaced chair's Vogue-ness as a specific function of its is-ness has been investigated. Is there any feature of the self that could meaningfully distinguish the self from others? Or is there any unique function that only I could perform as a form of equipment for others? The chair is "an other" with features unnecessary to its is-ness of Being-a-chair, but can we say the same about humans in their am-ness of Being-a-human?

Pragmatically and practically speaking: yes!

You don't need those arms and legs to continue being you. You can continue to be you with one kidney, one lung, half your liver, half your intestines, and even half of your brain! Your heart can be transplanted, your pituitary glands supplemented into obsoletion, and your bones replaced by either metal or hard prosthetic ones. The only things I can think of that are NOT replaceable with our current development of technology are things in the very center of the brain that are necessary to maintain vital function, like the pons, and that general area near the top of the spinal column. Those cannot be surgically replaced. But, we can still get pedantically microscopic and take even those areas out cell-by-cell and atom-by-atom, since not every cell nor atom contained within the pons are necessary for it to remain functioning as the pons. And every bit of our DNA can (and naturally does) become deleted and makes additions all the time. Every atom of our Being likewise adds Nothing to the whole of our individual am-ness.

But shall we say in this one instance that $0+0+0+0=1$? No, don't be preposterous. I am

Null. There is Nothing at the core of my am-ness. Every conscious thing that hears and un-derstands this logic simultaneously can affirm and negate its soundness. I cannot be Nothing while Being-in-active-thought. But I must be Nothing because no feature and no part of me is ontologically necessary for me to Be-as-I-am.

And this is the crux of Snavely's Conun-drum, the inescapable reductio ad absurdum of critical existential thought. I am [both, either, neither] Being [and, or, nor] Nothing. My am-ness is [also, possibly, not] Non-Being.

And because this reduction is inescapable at this point, it then follows that Everything-that-exists indeterminately-exists, perpetually and perfectly paradoxically is what it is not, as in its is-ness is its not-ness, the is-ness possibly is its not-ness, and its is-ness is not its not-ness. Yes, no, both, and neither. $1, 0, 0^0,$ & __. And so long as Everything-that-exists is not Nothing-that-exists, Nothing-that-exists exists-certainly.

But if Everything is Nothing (like the chair at the center of its Being is actually Non-Being), then even Nothing-the-thing also in-determinately exists. To reiterate this point, we've already deduced how a Non-Being can Be-the-First-Cause as a single QVB stuck between Being-a-point and not-Being-at-all. Thus, Every-Being indeterminately-exists just as the Non-Being also indeterminately-exists.

Shall I continue this meaninglessly meaningful rant? Not when I have Nothing-more to say to you!

...

"Nothing-more!"

...

Now what can we use to distinguish the nouns of Non-Being and not-a-being from the adjectives used to describe the is-ness of Nothingness? Nobody versus the empty void that surrounds Her, Nothing as the-thing-in-itself versus the post hoc attributes of Nothingness? I have hinted at this solution already, but let's go more in-depth.

It is what-it-is, which is its is-ness, which is the totality-of-attributes that are accurately and potentially attributable to 'it.' This totality-of-attributes is never fully known, but when consensus between subjects (i.e. peer-review) is reached concerning a thing-in-question, understanding of the thing increases, thus filling in our gaps of understanding it by adding to its is-ness.

Even if and when the meta-qualia-dimensional-analysis I am currently performing is complete, and each of those Dimensions is methodically measured and defined for a thing, that doesn't mean that its is-ness has reached its totality, since concernings of 'it' may lie beyond our current language constraints (only because it's impossible to reach infinite precision, especially for units of arbitrary measures like 'beauty' or 'Vogue-ness').

And even when its is-ness is as close to complete as reasonably possible (by measuring every finite dimension concerning a thing), there is still the concern of the thing's totality-of-involvements with Everything-else in Mass-Electric-Space-Time, and the new qualia values created from these totality-of-involvements!

Science as a whole then holds the potential to be majorly made up of attempts at winning the Ignobel Prize in mere hopes of accidentally stumbling upon new findings worthy of the Nobel Prize. I can see it now: "*The 2300 Nobel*

Prize goes to the successful lung transplant with a mycelium-infused rubber bath toy!"

No-thing can be fully known, but methodically sorting out its is-ness will get us as close to 'it' as we can get. And conversely, only Nothing can be fully known, because Nothing doesn't actually interact with Everything-that-exists, it is merely the medium Everything-that-exists exists in. And every conceivable and inconceivable negation and substantive dimension used to measure things in Mass-Electric-Space-Time-Quanta-Qualia for the Non-Being is 0, in the form of its self-negation as Being-as-Non-Being.

This indeterminacy about the nature of Nothing-as-Non-Being tells us Nothing about Nothing, which is simultaneously circular, tautologous, complete, and self-negating by our Being-as-Null-in-the-world-in-human-reality.

And since we bring the 0 into Being by our being aware of it, rather than leave the value space empty, so long as we acknowledge that the 0 exists only as a stand-in for the Non-existent empty Void, we can perhaps bring philosophy back full circle in demonstration of why and how *"I know that I know Nothing"* fully.

Nothing, in essence, is the totality-of-Non-involvements, the totality-of-Non-attributes, and is what it is not, which is Everything. (But mostly just the first 2 things). Shall I become a Tri-gnostic nihilist now? Knowing Nothing, No-thing, and ___? Probably not, because No-thing implies the emptiness of Every-concernful-thing within its context.

Thus, there are only 2 Nothing's to know, by which we can know Nothing fully: the total-lack-of-things (No-thing) and the thing-in-itself, by which all things which can be ne-gated are negated (Nothing). In this way, I also demonstrate how the Nothingness which is the First Cause, even while it is whole, is already split. Nothing's split-ness is part of its is-ness, just as its wholeness is part of its is-ness.

Since it is what it is, namely, Nothing, and it is what it isn't, namely Everything, Everything is Nothing, and it is also Not-Nothing. I don't think I require a further explanation that wasn't made clear in *The Gospel of Zilch & Nada* con-cerning my intimate explanations of the void, since they are self-negating and perhaps even based on baselessness, which is common for the well-reasoned to recognize the Non-reason within, and for the well-sensed to see the Non-sense at work.

But truly, I say to you, whatever is the rock of your understanding, be it God or science or Being-for-yourself-and-others or reason-in-itself, beneath that rock there is Nothing.

I will not negate these 4 rocks, for to do so may result in devastating disequilibrium to our collective society, and I fear that I may be too good of a sophist that I could succeed in doing so in the minds of others if I tried. To Zilch & Nada belong devotion, to science belongs knowledge, to Being-for-yourself-and-others belongs philanthropy, and to reason belongs meditations and self-discipline. I have negated Everything below these rocks, and many things above these rocks. But it may do society some good to recognize that the foundations of understanding are based on Nothing but the 'I' whose am-ness is the reflector of understanding.

Chapter 10

Critique of the Critique, the of, the Pure, and the Reason

And a lot of my work in the future, Zilch willing, will be in the further negation of notable things resting on those 4 rocks: devotions to God, science, philanthropy, and self-discipline. Sensei Snavely is a Master Negator, yes, Being-a-Master-Negator is a part of MY am-ness. Splendid! Now I shall say "Master Negator" 3 times really fast, just for amusement's sake, seeing that the English audiobook would make listeners hear words that sound like "masturbator." Ready? Here we go: Master Negator, Master Negator, Master Negator.

So I believe it would seem appropriate for me to take an active part in negating the two predecessor books in this multi-generational, multinational, and multi-language trilogy, and another tangentially related book, as to conclude this book in this order: 17th Century German Immanuel Kant's *Critique of Pure Reason,* 20th Century German Martin Heidegger's *Being and Time* (the first of our multi-thinker trilogy), & 20th Century Frenchman Jean-Paul Sartre's *Being and Nothingness* (the second of our trilogy), with a final meta-negation of *Non-Being and Nothingness* by this silly 21st Century English-speaking American.

To begin critiquing the *Critique of Pure Reason,* I see no reason to reason that the reason that is being critiqued is pure, as I've said already. For purity implies that only the thing-in-question exists within itself, as reason-in-itself. But what would reason alone even look like? Although I agree that space and time are *a priori* concepts, and I see that both of these dimensions are required for a reasoning reason to demonstrate Being-in-active-thought, is that enough for the rationale alone to label itself as "pure?" I don't think it is.

Earlier I brought to our collective reasoning the Quantum Vacuum Bit to demonstrate how all reason could reasonably reside within a 0-D point simulating what we call 'reasoning.' Thus, even these 2 fundamental *a priori* dimensions may be in error, assuming space and time where there is None via Nothing as a Non-Being QVB. And since this Hypothesis of there being a thing of pure reason is as Non-negatable as the Null Hypothesis that opposes it, the purity of the reason will always be a thing-in-question.

Once an *a priori* facet of knowledge is found or deduced, by what method can we test it for impurities? Shall we use the same method used to find the knowledge in the first place? Cannot we see this for the nonsense that it is? The claim of discovering nuggets of knowledge with reason alone, whilst using a reason that was produced after years of experience finding out which reasons were reasonable and which ones weren't.

May I make the same claim that I have

discovered pure Nothingness with Non-sense alone, whilst using Non-sense that took years of experience finding out which Non-senses were nonsensical and which ones weren't? Within the word, you can even see how the Non-sense parallels the pure reason, *which sought to remove all sensuous experiences from the reasonings!* Therefore, the pure reason that negates the experiences of the senses would be better labeled as Pure Non-sense from the git-go.

Beyond these things, I found myself annoyed by what I perceived to be an incessant need for order in Kant's mind, which sometimes led to tunneled thinking as opposed to critical thinking. For example, about 100 pages into my translation, Kant speaks of Aristotle's Table of Categories of Quantity, Quality, Relation, and Modality, and notes: *"In each class the number of categories is always the same, namely three."* He mistook the number of examples given within each class as the exhaustive number of examples each class was capable of providing. (And just to provide an additional example or two, we could add 'Equivalence' to

Relation, and 'Total Negation' and 'Emptiness' to Quantity).

He considered space and time to be under the new category of pure concepts but barred himself from doing so because (I assume) he thought it would ruin Aristotle's perfect order of three since the pure concept category would only have two. Perhaps if he rose from the dead to read *this* book, he would maintain his order of three by substantively adding Nothing to this pure concept class. But again, the pureness of even those three pure concepts would still be up for questioning; to determine if the rationale behind the questions is itself tainted with impurities. Pure and extraordinary sense is muddied by the senses, so to speak and, whilst we are alive beings-in-action, it's not like we can just become-blind-and-deaf-and-untasting-and-unsmelling-and-unfeeling-and-unbal-anced-for-the-purpsose-of-attaining-pure-reason. *It would literally be senseless to attempt such a feat.*

And concerning senselessness, it frustrates me to no end that both Kant and Heidegger, both of whom had a near-universal utility to add to the philosophical field, wrote their highest acclaimed works in such a way that it took over 200 pages for me to even begin to acknowledge their brilliance. I'm not saying that I think I'm THE standard for brilliance, but rather that I have already been influenced by Einstein in the sense that I believe *"if you cannot explain something simply, you don't understand it well enough."* And to me, it is senseless to over-complicate these relatively simple concepts introduced, even if it was the first time some of these concepts were introduced to that level of depth.

For Kant in particular, I had to put his book back on the shelf after 111 pages in pure frustration, inspiring me with the thought to make a video of me burning the book as the thumbnail, under the title of "Critique of Pure Garbage." Thankfully, I could not do that with a clear conscience without reading the whole thing, and thus, "Critique of Pure Garbage" was itself tossed away in my mind's trash bin after acknowledging that he started making sense after a gruesome 266 pages from my perspective in my translation.

In hindsight, Kant and I would agree on a few core issues, the main agreement being that empiricism and rationalism are both incomplete concerning their applicability to find the truths they set out to find. Empiricism lacks its ontological basis, relying on the observations of appearance to determine their truths, thus the core issue of Being is bypassed and ignored entirely. And the limits of rationalism are easy enough to lay out in full detail, that is, to say Everything pure reason could ever achieve, that I will stick it all at the end of this book like it was Nothing.

The transcendental middle ground between these two schools of thought is and has been the way of the scientific process since the Enlightenment. But as I have hopefully demonstrated adequately earlier in this work, where I differ from Kant is that if the concepts of space & time are *a priori*, then the concepts of at least one of the two matter dimensions of mass or electromagnetism would also be required to maintain their *a priori* validity as Being-ontologically-certain. Because without them to actualize different points of contact between space or the changes that occur over time, space & time themselves would be obsolete as being indistinguishable from Non-Space and Non-Time. As a matter of fact, pure mass and pure light cannot be observed independently, since mass is what's needed to resist the light from going through a would-be observer who could verify the action, but I digress.

To continue contrasting myself with Kant, I will present a full paragraph of his, and elaborate on how exactly transcendental empiricism works when it is literally based on Nothing in light of his observations.

"Thus we find that pure reason, which at first seemed to promise nothing less than expansion of our knowledge beyond all limits of experience, contains, if properly understood, nothing but regulative principles, which do indeed postulate greater unity than the empirical use of the understanding can ever achieve; yet, by the very fact that they place the goal which has to be reached at so great a distance, they carry the agreement of the understanding with itself, by means of systemic unity to the highest possible degree. But if they are misunderstood

*and mistaken for constitutive principles of tran-
scendent knowledge, they produce, by a brilliant
but deceptive illusion, persuasion and imaginary
knowledge, by thereby constant contradictions
and disputes."*

In other words, from his perspective, the knowledge obtained from science, even with the transcendental principles contained in the scientific method, would lead to a convincing set of pseudo-scientific knowledge. It's as if the reliability of replicable appearances means Nothing towards the pursuit of truth. It's as if sticking your head in the sand and ignoring the utility of *a posteriori* knowledge entirely is better than reason based on transcendental reason which is ultimately based on Nothing and get us Nowhere anyways!

But, if we start from Nothing from the git-go, and also, I admit, a transcendental philological method that defines the orders of reason within it, both the empiricists and the rationalists would benefit. Empiricists would finally, as they have merely presupposed so far, have an ontological basis for their knowledge, by relying on the Mass-Electric-Space-Time dimensions as the transcendental definition for the objective world that is Being. Each dimension is a continuum that contains the possibility and capacity for Being-ness to emerge in the world as action, for without them, all that would remain is Non-Being.

And rationalists would then, likewise, have a reason to stick their heads out of the sand, and use the sand to help make some concrete, so to speak. Once Nothingness, is truly known in its totality, as its simultaneous Non-Applicability and 0 magnitude for every substantive dimension, the systemic unity of a Dimensionalist system would then be capable of being tested with philological, mathematical, and physical means, rather than stick with the near-meaningless qualitative sand salads that have been the sustenance for wisdom since the dawn of man. Only then, can philosophy meaningfully progress, when it humbles itself to be critiqued and upheld by empirical methods.

Chapter 11

This bee be Non-Being or Being-dead?

Heidegger's *Being and Time* thankfully did not have these same strict issues Kant appeared to have. For what it is worth, I think Heidi did an excellent job of providing a solid ontological definition for his *Dasein*, albeit an unnecessarily over-complicated one. Using my words to summarize this work, *Dasein* is the is-ness of Being; the 'it' at the core of 'what it is.' And the latter third of the book proves to a reasonable degree that this *Dasein* exists (or is) in time, which I hope I made it easier to understand by noting how Being requires either real or potential action, which could only ever happen within time.

Just as the concept of running requires a runner to endure for a time, so does the concept of being require a *Dasein* to endure for a time. Even if I were to assert that the *Dasein* is ultimately Null, we would still be left with 'Null is Being, and enduring for a time.' Whether we assert that which is Being is something like *Dasein* or Null, it is irrefutable for the well-reasoned individual that it is ultimately a thing, even whilst Being-as-No-thing-in-particular.

So naturally where I diverge from Heidegger is rather than dismiss the possible negation of this thing-in-question, I embrace it, and even add it as a necessary ontological component of this thing-in-question. Its 'is-ness' is the positive assertion and explanation of the dipolar authenticity and inauthenticity aspect of the *Dasein*.

The concepts were simple to understand in this book, but frustrating, because Heidegger appeared to have a tendency to really build up to what he was about to say rather than just say it. It led to frustrations and thoughts that were left incomplete for several hundred pages, which in real-world-reading-time took well over a month to complete, in its soundness in my mind.

For example, around page 98 of my translation, he speaks of the 'ready-to-hand' as a totality of equipmentality that had already been discovered (not a direct quote), which any critically thinking mind would deduce is impossible to do. Calculating Every-probable-action, and discovering them for a single piece of equipment would take the rest of time to discover. And it wasn't until page 191 that it was clarified that *"this totality need not be grasped explicitly by a thematic interpretation."* 93 whole pages of me assuming it did, since that is what 'discovery' implies.

And on a somewhat unrelated note that just happened to show up next in my notes on the book, Heidi's hyper use of hyphens to an absurd level may have inspired the even more absurd hyper use of hyphens in this book. I believe his longest streak was 8 words long, in which he used the phrase *"Being-just-present-at-hand-and-no-more,"* to describe a recently deceased person who is 'Being-no-longer-in-the-world.' Once I read that, I knew I had to increase this absurdity on several fronts, even if my editor didn't like it so much even after she read this explanation as a meta-joke for philosophers.

And Sartre even added to this unnecessary absurdity using this 10-word long streak: *"being-in-the-midst-of-the-world-for-the-other."* So for this existential trilogy, it was only fitting that I include the serious common phrase, the 9-word 'Being-in-the-world-alongside-us-in-human-reality,' and the ridiculously long 129-word that involved tacos and Frank's hot sauce. Psychologically speaking, I would guess that this particular mode of absurdity stems from the attempts at finding meaning beyond the ontological bare minimum of Being-in-itself.

This rut of philosophy, observed by outsiders as an indication of death and a 'dead field of study' may likely have its roots in the overwhelming majority embrace of Being as the primary means to build the field further, whilst also rejecting the Cartesian mode of examining both the physical and metaphysical features of the thing-in-question that the rest of the Hierarchy of Sciences depend on. It gives me this vision of 2 cavemen philosophers having this absolute strawman of a conversation, that all in all, really isn't too far from the truth.

"I found meaning!"

"*Grunts* Yes, do tell!"

"Meaning is Being!"

"*beats chest* Yes is! Say more!"

"Ugh... Being implies... A BEING!"

"*Hits head with a coconut* A Being?! What is a Being doing?"

"*slides in closely, and sensuously whispers in ear* Being."

"*ejaculates in ecstasy* Meaning is a Being Being! Does a Being have another a Being, or a Being alone?"

"*stops to ponder* Hmm... Me no know. Maybe a Being Being alone together with I."

"*eats a banana peel* One, I Being. Two, a Being Being. Therefore, 2 Beings be Being!"

"*throws the remaining banana fruit into the face of the peel eater* Not 2 Beings! 3!"

"*slips into a happy coma for 1 second, to arise and be amazed. 3?!"

"Yes! One, I Being. Two, Our a Being Being. Three, we all Being-in-the-world! The World be Being Three!"

"No, a Being Being implies a world for a Being to be Being in. The World in the '-ing' of Being!"

"Aye, hand over coconut... *hits head with coconut, busting the coconut open* But can Being just Be? Or just Be be Non-Being?"

"*gets stung by a bee* *extinguishes the life from the bee* This bee be Non-Being!"

"No! This bee be Being by Being-dead!"

I could go on for pages more, but I think I've made my point. This strawman imaginary exchange that has appeared to go on for about a century could have been avoided by elaborating on the features that are required for a Being to be a Being. Moving beyond the bare-minimum verbs and nouns, use adjectives and prepositions to create meaningful relational connections, and actually investigate how it is and what dimensions are useful to describe and distinguish between these different modes of being. Can ontology still be a basis for a future Cartesian Dimensionalism? Absolutely, for then we can allow these dimensions, especially the ontologically necessary ones for Being in the first place; the ones that allow us to be Being-in-action; Mass-Electric-Space-Time phenomena, to be the fundamental basis for elaboration on what beings are doing.

We, and by we I mean 'Everything,' express our Being by the fundamental interactions of these 4 necessary dimensions that hold/maintain certain properties inherently, and others prescribed after the fact. Without these 4 dimensions interacting the way they do, our Being would be indiscernible from Non-Being.

Using Heidegger's analogy, the hammer's features don't make the hammer, but the ability to use the hammer as equipment makes the hammer. But where we, and by we I mean 'the global society of critical thinkers,' must continue, is in recognizing this same hammer can only ever truly begin Being-a-hammer within the confines of its common contextual background in-the-world. The hammer doesn't exist in a vacuum! The primal language of grabbing the hammer and using it as a hammer as equipment that is ready-to-hand cannot be done without taking the time to close the space between yourself and the hammer, grasping it in your Mass-Electric-Space-Time hands, and move the mother-fucking hammer in relation to other objects in-the-world with Force, which is Mass*Space/Time^2!

The dimensions aren't just in the background of the world, but within the very fabric of our Being-in-the-world, and in each other's Being-in-the-world-alongside-us-in-human-reality, which includes the hammer. We move the hammer into action, we move our bodies into action, we move our thoughts into active thought, and really, this is telling us Nothing new that we have recognized since we were children.

Why does it take big-Null brains to push us forward in such an obvious manner? To move beyond Being, get out of our heads so to speak, and genuinely explore the world and the universe? To not stop at "we are here," but to continue the definition of here, and ask "what's over there?" To be as clear as reasonably possible: I am not saying that the dimensions have an ontological necessity for our very Being since I have already said that the dimensions manifest as features of our am-ness that add Nothing new or necessary to our Being. What I am saying, is that the dimensions DO have an ontological necessity for the world-itself that holds our Being, and this is an ontological necessity for our Being-in-the-world-in-human-reality.

The 'time' that Heidegger observed we are being 'in' is both a dimension and feature that, in addition to space and matter, are necessary for meaningful actions and relations to occur in-the-world-alongside-us-in-human-reality. Matter's Mass-Electric dimensions can now finally be justified as necessary features of the world, because if all that existed was I (a Null thing), space, and time, then space, time, and the world would disappear since there would be no other point-of-reference for any action in-the-world to take place at all. So the mass and electric dimensions are themselves the distinguishing points of contact amidst space and time that allow action to take place in the first place.

This logic shows how these Primary

Dimensions are co-dependent on each other: Space-Time requires the Mass-Electric to be either reasonably-distinguished or empirically-observed in-the-world, and the Mass-Electric requires Space-Time to begin Being-in-action-in-the-world. And because my actions are distinct from your actions in-the-world, and your actions can thwart, obstruct, and possibly even stop my actions, your Being to me as an 'other,' and any Being to you as an other is as certain, nay, is indistinguishable from the world-in-itself. (We ARE the world!) The world's is-ness is our collective-am-ness, which is our are-ness. We-are-Beings-in-action-in-and-as-Mass-Electric-Space-Time-in-and-as-the-world-amongst-outselves-in-human-reality-until-we-are-Non-Being.

You are what I am not, and I am not what you are, and we are here. Together we are One, even whilst alone I am None. We are Mass-Electric-Space-Time, and we are Null. We are Everything split, and we are Everything whole. We are going our own ways, and we are going Nowhere in particular. And I know that I know Nothing and that this knowledge will help us understand ourselves as Everything better. We are not the dimensions in themselves, but we are the points that make up the dimensions of the world. We grab ourselves by the mass, see ourselves by our light and distance ourselves from ourselves in an effort to go our own ways with whatever time we have, our are-ness is the world.

Can I, after all this, go back to Heidegger? What else can I say? That the magnum opus didn't make for an easy read until page 274? Or that his statement on page 266 that *"every uncoveredness is an uncoveredness of some-thing"* made me think of Scooby-Doo's headless horseman having 20 masks on only to reveal the real headless horseman was, in fact, the real headless horseman the whole time, to dem-onstrate how only the multiplicity of useless masks was demonstrated? Or that his saying *"Temporality is the reason for the clock,"* was taken from the handbook of Captain Obvious? No, I don't think much more needs to be said in this medium. He was an inspiration of his time and still is several generations later, and without him, neither Satre's book nor this one would have been made possible. But I do not envy the scholars of Heidi in the slightest, due to his overly complicated language.

Nietzsche is the better writer from what I've read, and I can only hope to compare to his (Nietzsche's) timeless wit if I fail to go beyond it. The brevity of this work, even amidst its intentionally unnecessary redundancies, hopes to be a welcoming relief compared to the headaches endured whilst reading long-winded philosophers like Heidegger.

Chapter 12

Being the negation of the negation of The Negation

But for now, I will move on to Sartre. Contrary to popular opinion I do consider that the Frenchman was on the right track on where to progress from Heidegger. After all, we both think somewhat Cartesianally, and both take the topics of Nothing & radical centrism seriously. There were many times that I found myself discouraged from writing this book, because a lot of his existential observations were dead-on-target, and I have no desire to steal a profound thinker's thunder if I had Nothing useful to add to the thunderclap.

For example, his observation that *"Nothingness cannot be nothingness without nihilating itself explicitly as the nothingness of the world."* was a novel concept to me. The active mode of negation even of itself is an inherent attribute of the void. It was an absolutely fascinating thought to deposit into my brain bank. What else would that mean to me, other than our Being honors the futile sacrifice of the Void's Self-Nullification?

It also came to my attention that Sartre's negations and self-negations in "not being" actually don't negate Heidegger's use of "Being," as was intended. Not being is still a mode of Being, namely Being-what-it-is-not. (Don't get me wrong, Sartre's observations are phenomenally self-consistent, even if they aren't ontologically consistent with what Heidi was saying.)

But I will say in criticism, that Sartre has undergone the tendency to make assertions without adequately backing them up. *(Even if I perhaps also tend to have this problem, it's hard not to be when there isn't exactly any peer-reviewing going on at the moment.)* For example, there was this passage saying the woman who was sexually dissatisfied was at fault for *'divorcing her object from her subject,'* or something like that, rather than postulating that the man may have had a part to play as well, namely, being-not-good-at-the-sex. A hypothesis asserted by the questionable practices of Freudian psychoanalysis does not adequately question the Null Hypothesis nor other substantiated hypotheses.

There was also this paragraph full of unnecessary and petty tautologies. I should probably parody it and be even more precise than I was earlier, by saying X is not X, because the first X is conceived at a different time, therefore every X is a different X! So we can say that although equivalence can be approximately demonstrated within the world, absolutely true equivalence amongst the multitude of things, to make sense, must exist beyond Mass-Electric-Space-Time and not within it.

But moving on to page 139 of *Being and Nothingness*, there was this small statement that got me thinking: *"For it is only by means of *a lack that a lack can come from being."* I think all I need to do here for commentary here is provide a counterexample. Like, I have a sack of spoiled potatoes, but I lack safe food. Thus from the potatoes being-spoiled-potatoes did a lack of edible food arise.

And on page 263 of my translation, I got really riled up and spent way too much time reflecting on it. When Sartre says: *"A quality cannot be objectified if it is subjective,"* I say the object is subjectified. If there is consensus between subjects about the objective dimensions of the object, then the quality of a particular shade of color (subjective) can be demonstrated to have one or more electromagnetic wavelengths interacting with different intensities (objective).

And when he said *"It is the lemon's acidity that is yellow,"* I didn't hold back from an acerbic tone myself, and considered the statement spoken by a moron. Simply because he was attributing one kind of descriptor for another, and actually, attributing charge to wavelength. It's a false equivalence to say the lemon is acidic, and the lemon is yellow, therefore acidic is yellow. Using only two different dimensions of the lemon used to explain the totality of the lemon is wrong. Even the same dimension of color shows this error for multi-colored objects: Cow is white, and the same cow is black, therefore white is black.

And at last, when his words were translated to say *"the jam's sticky coldness is a revelation of its sweet taste to my fingers,"* I had to give a hearty laugh. This guy has clearly never felt and tasted any remnants of the Early 21st Century Slime Craze which would clearly expose the sticky coldness revelation to be revealing Nada about the cold and sticky thing's sweetness! Reason with me here! So long as something is, the parts of its is-ness are small and cumulative to the whole thing-in-question. When talking about Nothing, we can say Zilch is Nada, but when Nothing is Something, as 0^0 things, we cannot say the parts of the thing-that-is-Being are Null. Otherwise, the is-ness of Null would be its own is-not-ness. *(I am aware this appears to contradict what I said earlier, about its is-ness is what it is not, but it doesn't. To elaborate, Being, in this work, is indeterminate between*

Being-absolute (1) and Non-Being (0). The totality of is-ness that is knowable is as close to Being-absolute that we can get, where all that remains is Non-Being, but it cannot be known that we know it 100%, because the relational attributes of other things also need to be known in full as well for Being-absolute to emerge for a thing. So really, No-thing can be known fully (which leaves parts of a thing's is-ness to be desired), but Nothing cannot be known fully (which is a thing's is-not-ness in its totality).)

Chapter 13

THIS IS IT!

Now, I hate to talk about this, but Sartre begs me from beyond his grave to do it. This is so important compared to all that, that it transcends that to be this! The this-ness is the is-ness that is its it-ness, there is no doubt about it. It is beyond the capability of being doubted, this is certain, it cannot be made any clearer than this. For if it was any less clear, it would be that, and that would be outrageously absurd.

THIS IS IT! Not as an anticipatory 'is' as a linking verb in time, but an equivocation 'is' that tells it like it is! It is so certain, that Nothing, nay, not even Nothing is capable of negating it. In all seriousness, if it was not this, then it would be that. Can it be both this and that? Absolutely, because I just said so, like a distinguished Nada Doctorate of Philosophy.

But, now this is important, because even though this is not that, and this is it, it is also that, making it the certain commonality between this and that. Is it Nothing? Possibly, we would be foolish to negate the possibility so soon. Could it being-Nothing be true? If and only if that is false, to make it true that falsehoods have Nothing in-common with truth and pure reason. That is it if it is false. And that is all I have to say about that.

But if that's the case then this couldn't be further from the truth! Is this a lie worth believing? If it is the case that that is the case, where does that leave this? Shall we leave this to its own devices? As if we had any other choice, which we do. Either this is true, or that is true, or it is true (making both this and that true), or Nothing is true, (making both this and that false) or *it* is Nothing is true, which makes Nothing important, which makes it important as well, which makes this and that importantly unimportant.

Is that all? No. Is this and that all? Of course not. But is this and that it? Yes, but incompletely so. Is this, that, and the other *it* and *not it?* So long as the other is Null, yes. Is this the other? No, it's that. Is the other all of that? Yes.

Shall I go on with this? I could, but I'd rather move on to that. That is if you will allow me such a luxury to skip over to its end. And the Lord Zilch says, "It is finished." And the Jesus Christ Null also said: "It is finished." But the Nully Spirit says to you, *"It's not over yet!"* Its Non-sense endures forever. Ramen.

But is it under?... I'm just kidding, I'm done now. But commenting on Sartre isn't, and that is where we shall continue. Between pages 391-394 of his 811-page-chonky-boi, I had a vision! A silly vision of me getting on a stage, and demonstrating my shamelessness and consideration-for-the-Other, by allowing those who would feel shamed upon seeing my nakedness to leave, to demonstrate my being without shame. But in this section, Sartre appears to think such a demonstration would be an act of pride, namely projectionally saying some-thing like, *"I aim to make use of this beauty or strength or intelligence that [the other] confers on me insofar as [they] constitute me as an object in order to assign to [them], be reversing the direction of flow, a passive feeling of admiration or love,"* saying elsewhere that such shameless-ness would be *"already a reaction of flight [of shame for being an object] and bad faith."* To say shame is completely Non-negatable is just weird within the context of the rest of his book.

Now to his credit, around my translations pages 415-416, Sartre appeared to be saying, as I've already said more clearly, that the dimen-sions of an object are indistinguishable from the dimensions of the world, by saying exactly, and I quote, *"But it is we ourselves who decide on these dimensions through our very arising in the world, and we have to decide on them, otherwise they would not be at all...Pure knowl-edge would in effect be knowledge without any point of view, and therefore a knowledge of the world that was necessarily situated outside the world. But that has no meaning: the knowing being would only be knowledge, as he would be defined by his object, and his object would disappear within the complete lack of distinction of reciprocal relations. Thus knowledge can only be something that arises for someone engaged within a determinate point of view…"* (in other words, within the world; within Mass-Electric-Space-Time) *"…that he is…That is an ontological necessity."*

This is so eloquently insightful, and I happily reproduce it to give credit where it is due. I don't even have any words to add to it, it was so on-point.

But nearing page 431, my frustration as a psychologist with the philosopher reached a boiling point, so I shall aid both fields by providing a reasonable defense of the existing ontology required to uphold the field of psychology as it is. *(Since it appears that this kind of thinking has thoroughly permeated all fields of modern science).* Assuming I understood Jean-Paul correctly, he seemed to adamantly dismiss psychological subjectivity as the primary means of understanding objective phenomena with perception. I say that it is in fact this dismissal that leads to what he called *"a paradox of a physical instrument being handled by a mind."* All sensations that are perceived are connected to the brain via the central nervous system. The body is the neurons and the nerves, and the mind is merely the interpretation of what the sensations mean, which is ambiguous.

This is the extent to which distinguishing consciousness from the brain is useful, precisely because beyond this distinction, *the mind IS the brain!* And the nervous system assists the brain in sensing phenomena to help decide which actions would be most beneficial in maintaining Equilibrium. Even the self-reflective and self-aware process of consciousness can be readily observed to still require these neurons' ability to communicate with each other. Although some forms of consciousness being detached from the body as a sensory experience are not completely devoid of evidence themselves, their frequency in occurrences is too infrequent to be deemed a reliable truth to adhere to.

This sort of thinking showed up again, when Sartre said, *"The psychologists ought to have asked themselves what sort of ontological structure could belong to a phenomenon that is acquainted with what it is by something that has not yet come to be."* In making such an onto-logical structure clear, as if others haven't done so already, the thought processes behind active imagination ontologically requiring active neu-rons to extrapolate future likely but uncertain possibilities is all that is required here. Behavior doesn't require ontology below action-in-itself, since actions must be physical to be-in-the-world.

However, to appease the likes of Sartre, the full answer to the question he proposed that psychologists ask themselves, is stated here to be *the actions of neurons communicating with each other from which new actions are per-formed in the world* is the ontological basis for psychology. If actions are observed in the world, they can and should be tested and stud-ied rigorously to more fully grasp the is-ness of the phenomenon in question, which are actions originating from a complex neural network.

Or did I not understand the question at hand? Surely, I didn't misunderstand.

Chapter 14

Sartre Part 3: Revenge
of the Hammer

Nearing the end of Sartre's book, and perhaps now my own as well, his breaking of the dyad of *doing* and *having* as a fundamental basis for actions made me want to *do* and *have* a burger, a woman, a cow, and a job. I see what he was saying, as *doing* includes actions from a self, and *having* includes actions concerning others, and all other actions are characterized by their negation of *not doing* and *not having*. Whether these actions of *doing* or *having* are coherent with reality or not is still up for debate, which I intend to do here.

Is anything in the world capable of being had as a possession, or is possession an emergent property of spatial-temporal proximity of equipment being ready-to-handle as equipment? Being capable of manipulating other objects as your will tells it to move is what it means to be *having* so far as I can tell. And could this not negate the need for *having* at all? If I *have* a woman, doesn't this mean I tell her what she could and should be *doing*? I would be *doing* my authoritative duty of commanding, and the woman, if she complies, would be *doing* what I said.

Similarly, in the case of the hammer, in it being-an-obstinate-yet-compliant-inanimate-object, requires either me or another more-compliant object to *do* the act of gripping the hammer by the handle to get the hammer to begin the action of *doing* the hammering. In this case, I would not be hammering, I would simply be forcing an obstinate hammer into *doing* the act of hammering for me. That is just a function of me *doing* my job: being an Overman to the hammer, to the burger, to the willing subject, and to the subjugated subject.

In essence, to be *having* something implies the capacity for the thing to be *doing* what I desire it to do either now or sometime in the future.

Where else is there to go from here? If Nothing did exist, as a First Thing to exist, that would provide us with Nothing to base our own existence on. A lattice of Non-Beings all the way up and down the scales of the magnitude of the universe, as maddening as the thought is, would still be consistent with empirical observations. What I mean is that every Non-Being would then be Being-a-0-Dimensional-point on a 1-Dimensional string, and they interconnect by forming a lattice at the smallest scales. At intermediate scales, mereological nihilism negates things down to no part of them being necessary for things to be-as-they-are, which leaves Nothing as Non-Being as this necessary part for things to be-as-they-are. And at the cosmic scale, the universe as a whole, with this model, is being calculated by a Quantum Vacuum Bit.

Only our current awareness of these things cannot be negated, even if they aren't to be believed, but even our awareness will be negated one day in time, regardless if you believe it or not. Our actions define our way of being and permeate our Being despite the void, by using our distinct substantive points of contact composed of Mass-Electric-Space-Time to act with other actors Being-in-the-world-alongside-us-in-human-reality.

And the ideological pit of solipsism could only be maintained if the 'I' reading this was themselves a Non-Being QVB or QLB, to justify their awareness that requires Being-in-active-thought. However, the world as observed is more justifiable as being a negation of the Negator, as an inevitable possibility of Nothingness naturally negating itself. Existential meaning and purpose, if it is to survive, should likewise transcend the void of Non-Beings like our own Being, for if it doesn't, the void is surely capable of negating it.

Life is active, so we move. Meaning doesn't move; it simply defines what it is, which is its is-ness. Purpose, as meaning, should motivate us to action, to define what it means to live. But since meaning doesn't move the thing by itself, ironically enough, the meaning itself is just another form of Non-Being. And since we need meaning to define whatever it is in the first place, the is-ness of what meaning is, at least in part, is one of Non-Being as well.

This is in part why we Beings must give ourselves purpose, or have purpose be delegated to us by others. For if we don't, such an ideological pit will likely become indistinguishable from an existential pit, and the only logical conclusion to the question *"to be or not to be?"* would be the latter.

I defined Non-Being in this book; I gave the inherently meaningless meaning. And a Being being-in active-thought can do this for themselves, so... what does it mean for you to be? An active definition that grows with time as knowledge increases may be necessary for our continued conquest and subjugation of the Non-Being.

Chapter 15

The Non-Axiom's
Philological Structure

In addition, as I promised I'd do earlier, I need to point out one more error of Kant's which I'd like to disagree with in particular, even if it does hold to reason as it is. He said, *"Philosophy, therefore, is without axioms, and can never put forward its* a priori *principle with absolute authority, but must first consent to justify its claims by thorough deduction."*

Axioms are imaginary, but their construction and connections can and should be able to reflect the things which are in question by their is-ness. Yet still, to begin stating such a proposition, there is but one axiom in philosophy from which the rest of philosophy may rest, and that is the Non-axiom. It states Nothing in particular, but it states this Nothing with absolute authority.

To presuppose Nothing is as close to a presuppositionless axiom that philosophy, as an art of reflection, can grasp, with as much or more certainty and authority than "I am Being" holds. And on that note, I will now begin the full extent of pure reason that can be built from the smallest set of presuppositions laid out clearly, that begins with the Non-axiom, and asks a reasonably exhaustive list of questions to explore and connect with other axioms with certainty, so far as the questions themselves are deemed valid.

To presuppose Nothing is as close to pure reason as reason can achieve. I wish it was possible to hold absolutely 0 underlying axioms in a philological structure, but at least 1 is always required to make any sense beyond Non-sense. This 0th axiom should be vacant, but that would gain us Nothing and get us Nowhere, and we'd still be left with the same problem.

Beyond Nothing being presupposed, I will take the liberty to allow what I call "pure reason" to take me as far as possible, and ignore any nonsensical negations that could arise, like 0 is not Zero (thus, equivalence between qualitative and quantitative systems is reasonably supposed) and Nothing is not Zilch or 0 is not 00.00 (thus, equivalence between synonyms is granted and supposed for simplicity). Of course, equivalence in itself as an achievable thing is also presupposed, along with the many other logical and mathematical rules invoked on this journey. I will also avoid any meta answers that would just be me Being-a-smartass like "I am thinking." or "Hi thinking, I'm dad."

Reason-in-itself would be flawed to ignore the void that lies underneath it to skip to performing more substantial things like playing Minecraft or thinking about ontological empiricism.

1. What is [ ]?

First off, anything that is attempted at being identified (including [ ]) could possibly be in error due to deception or a lack of awareness of what the identifying thing is. The annoying thing about this is, if [ ] is a deception for something substantive, we would still know No-thing about what it is, that is until the unveiling of the truth is disclosed. Plus, under the circumstance that [ ] is not Nothing, it would cease to be [ ] and start being [whatever it is].

Not to mention that whatever truth is disclosed about [whatever it is] may itself be a deception that turns out to be Nothing anyways. So far as [ ] is [ ] as identified within the scope of pure reason, it truly is Nothing, but the possibility of deception with concerns of identity is unavoidable as negations of what they are. [ ], the subject of primary inquiry, is either Nothing and No-thing as the void and emptiness or a deception of something as an unknown Thing.

To investigate [ ] as Nothing and No-thing, we observe space in-itself. Space allows us the ability to see how it can be infinitely divided into smaller points and segments. But when all that remains is no space, as a 0-D point, that point is simultaneously there amidst the surrounding space, and missing as well, since it lacks all hints of dimensionality. 0 points are indistinguishable from a single point, thus they are equivalent when observed in isolation, as we are doing. Therefore, Nothing split between 0 0-D points and 1 0-D point is equal to the Nothing whole as [ ], which is Non-Being in its totality.

2. What is [ ] doing?

If [ ] is a deception, the probable actions of [ ] would then be vastly increased. The true actions of [ ] would be unknowable though, due to its appearance as [ ]. Even though Nothing is doing No-thing, if it is in fact Nothing, it should be noted that this is not in contradiction to Nothing being both split and whole, since no action is performed by Nothing to become split. It is merely capable of being observed in both states from the start.

An absolute 0 divided into 2, 3, or an infinite quanta of segments as Non-segments is equivalent to the whole/absolute 0 that isn't divided. Save for our *a priori* observations of it, they are equivalent. This is what I mean when I say I am a '*bi-gnostic*' nihilist. We can know (gnostic) that the void is both (bi) split and whole so long as we also uphold the transcendental philological structures of mathematics which bring us to this solution.

3. Who is [ ]?

It is Nobody and No-body. A Non-entity. 'Who' as a mode of inquiry implies a consciousness, which if transposed onto [ ], is an indeterminate presupposition. Thus, this line of thinking can go no further without an additional presupposition, which goes beyond pure reason.

4. How many [ ] are there?

If [ ] is purely imaginary, there are 0. If [ ] exists imprecisely as 0, there are infinitely many with this proof. For the function, $0/(n)$, every non-zero integer, irrational, and complex number will provide a satisfactory 0 as the output.

The empty set would then be filled with a whole lot of Nothing, with an infinite number of ways of expressing the grand total of 0 things in the set. The ability to count [ ] can transcend [ ] as well, which would sound like "one empty set, two empty sets, three empty sets, ..." and so on.

Also, 1 [ ] gives us 1, and the splitting of [ ] into No-thing and Nothing gives us 2. It's hard to avoid the nonsense that comes from asking this question since its answer wholly depends on how exactly we count it. Likewise, if we were to attribute Every-thing in the universe to a respective n in the function $0/(n)$, it can be seen to make even the proposition that "Everything is Nothing" sensible enough to not immediately dismiss as pure nonsense.

5. What is [ ] not?

Although we can ironically state "Nothing is Nothing" with certainty if and when it is truly Nothing, we cannot state that Everything is Nothing with the same certainty. Intuitively, the answer to the question is "Everything and any-thing, the Full set, the universe, and reality." But a presupposition would need to be added here in the same way that all identifying questions must presuppose. Either we suppose Everything is Nothing to affirm the Null Hypothesis which bets on the possibility of deception, or Everything is not Nothing to affirm substantive hypotheses, including the likely position of energy being the foundation of our Being.

6. Where is [ ]?

Either Nowhere, beyond, or within

space as a 0-D point that is Everywhere. Although all 3 of these options can be concurrent without contradiction, they aren't necessary, so [ ] may then be at none of those spaces. The Nowhere option implies the possibility of [ ] Being-a-figment-of-my-imagination.

The 0-D point being Everywhere gives [ ] the observed quality of being omnipresent, as an indeterminate possibility compared to being non-present in Nowhere.

7. When is [ ]?

Either Nowhen, before, after, or within time as a 0-D point. Just like space, and really, any dimensional clarification of [ ]'s is-ness, all 4 of these options can be correct without contradiction.

They aren't necessary, and [ ] may be at none of these times. The possibility of Nowhen implies the possibility of [ ] Being-a-figment-of-my-imagination as well. The [ ] as a 0-D point being beyond the constraints of time can give this Nothing the observed quality of being Everywhen, omnitemporal, and eternal as an indeterminate possibility compared to [ ] being only immobile in Nowhen.

8. Why [ ]?

Either no purpose, no knowable purpose, or inevitable. Purpose in general is not inherent, and meaning is defined by the subjects' reasoning. Thus, it takes time and effort to find purpose. And since [ ] lies beyond time, its purpose can never be found for-itself. So it is up to Beings-in-time to give [ ] its purpose if any is to be given to it at all. But there is no one definitive answer to give this question, to both [ ] and any possible thing you could put within it.

In this manner, it can and has been demonstrated that even when inquiring about anything outside one's own self-reflective awareness, the incompleteness of our perfect knowledge of it will be perpetual. Even when these questions are posed to our own object-thing, the same incompleteness problem emerges, in the sense that the answer to the question wouldn't be a complete description of what the question is asking. So the only certainty can come from the following question.

9. Who is reasoning about [ ]?

I am aware that I am aware of [ ] being the focus of my attention. Not knowing anything more about myself, even if it was a deceived awareness, would not negate the awareness itself. I am aware, I am conscious, and I have an active thinking process concerning myself with [ ]. All others' awareness and [ ]'s awareness adds a presupposition that the world as a mere appearance is or is not a certain way. I actively think, therefore I am. I must be Being, for I cannot not be whilst being in active thought. Even if the reasoning process was merely a mis-attribution of actions as thought, the change of actions underlying the reasoning that discriminates one thought from the next absolutely affirms the energy underlying the action underlying the thought itself.

But the possibility of I also being [ ] isn't a negated possibility, if and only if I am a Quantum Bit of Energy that is itself Spaceless, Timeless, Immaterial, etc., seeing that I could have set up a sort-of simulation with my Energy, and made it a part of the programming to forget that I alone was the one deceiving myself from the nature of my solitary reality.

In summary, all measurable inquiries, particularly when asking 'When?' concerning time, 'Where?' concerning space, and 'How?' concerning the totality of dimensions working together, these questions can only be elaborated on after presupposing that the appearance is how the thing-in-question really is. Of course, even when speaking of the 3 fundamental axioms that can be held with 0 additional presuppositions, namely, 'the Non-axiom,' 'I am,' and 'Being as Energy in Action,' these things would need a stable point of reference whilst Being-in-the-world to be known or used.

And since we know we need 2 points to make any line, if I lack determinate pointedness for both the Non-Being-as-Nothing and for Being-as-Energy-in-Action-for-anything-and-Everything-in-the-world inductively points towards a substantive hypothesis of Absolute Relativity being the only form of a viable Theory of Everything that could ever hope to hold water atop these 3 fundamental axioms. *(It is Absolute because there is no such stable point of reference to refer to.)*

Shoot, even these 3 axioms stand in opposition to each other! If No-thing was the First Cause, then the Non-Being could only be imaginary, as $0i$ *in its entirety*, but this contradicts the consistency of the quantitative system which we swore to uphold.

If Everything lacks Nothing, would it not still be outside Everything as I've already said?

And the possibility of I Being-Everything and/ or Being-Nothing-as-a-Non-Being, although reasonably unlikely, cannot both be completely negated simultaneously. It's like a pesky whack-a-mole that if you hit one, the other immediately pops up, and if you try to hit both, they both resist adding to your score.

All of the 'What?' questions as an attempt to identify what the thing-in-question is, can always possibly be a deception. And all of the 'Who?' questions add a presupposition of implied consciousness, with the sole exception of the question "Who is thinking about Being and Non-Being?," whilst 'I am' is actively thinking about these topics.

And lastly, the 'Why?' questions, as demonstrated by most 5-year-olds, can always be followed up with another *"Why?"* or *"Why not?"* to the point of reaching Nothing or a complete Non-answer. Since meaning (as a definition) cannot be fully reached without appeals to some standardized dimension of Being, any attempt to achieve Meaning will be left either existentially futile, nihilistically empty, paradoxically absurd, or under the guise of deception.

This deduction made me realize that all questions are in pursuit of the same Meaning, and grasping it is found, albeit incompletely, precisely by the asking process. A solid axiomatic system can easily show how Y follows X when the connecting questions are presented as well, and the other possibilities are at least briefly acknowledged and attempted to be rebutted. A Non-sequitur then can be defined by an incomplete axiomatic chain, where no single question can connect two propositions.

The set of propositional axioms before leading to a desired united conclusion, to hold a solid argument, should lead to a single outcome as well, and if it doesn't, another propositional axiom is required.

Chapter 16

"Uh...what the heck
did I just read?"

Final Round! Meta-critique of Non-Being!

Let's investigate a consistent scale for viewing how Non-Beings fill up all of space. Building up the smallest Bits of Energy needed to be a part of the world. 0-D Non-Being looking vaguely looking like [.], and a 1-D of Non-Beings looking like [. . . . .]. If more Non-Beings were placed in a 2-D grid, it would be most efficiently spaced as an equilateral triangle of points connecting 3 Non-Perpendicular strings of lines to comprise the 2-D grid.

As I continue to think about this problem, a

paradox of infinite divisibility arises. The question goes, *"How many 0-D points can surround a 0-D point?"* In 1-D space, the answer is obviously "2," but in 2 dimensions, the connection between the point and every other point would create another 0-D point infinitesimally adjacent to the previous, creating an entire circle's worth of points surrounding the central point, making the answer "infinite." But when the point is treated as an existent circle in the first place, the answer is "6" for 2-D and "12" for 3-D, with the point being an existent sphere.

Upon even further deduction, the stable 6-string grid for 3-D space connecting every point to the adjacent points would still leave us with gaps smaller than the points in between where smaller points could fit. So this empty space between the strings should be accounted for, to solve the paradox that would actually allow an infinite amount of strings to relationally connect every within-universe point of contact to every other. Because if this space isn't accounted for, there would be Nothing holding the strings in place to form a consistent natural structure, nor would there be any reason for both smaller string structures in-total and other completely separated string structures to be intertwined within these empty spaces.

I admit that if space is empty, things can still flow through the world. But then what would stop things (such as light) from leaving the world? That would make the space require a string barrier to not leak energy, which, as far as the world is concerned, is indistinguishable from annihilating it.

God and Nothing *could* fill these literal and physical gaps, but if there is a completely natural explanation without paradoxes arising, such a substantial string theory would be perpetually incomplete. But strings of Non-existent Non-Beings can both take the universe and say that the structure within is all we care of explaining, with the simultaneous acknowledgment that there is No-thing preventing the universe Being-a-point within another universe infinitum, as well as the points and their respective gaps from within our universe contain even smaller Non-Beings that fill in those gaps infinitum.

But that is some absurd Non-natural Non-falsifiable Non-sense Non-fitting for a theory-of-Everything-that-is-not-Nothing. Should I continue with these madness-inducing visions of circles within the gaps of other packed grids of other circles? The zoom-out reminds me that I am Null, I am 0. The zoom-in reminds me that from the perspective of an infinitesimal Being, I am an Infinite Somethingness, I am infinity.

The makeup of the fundamental Nothing-ness being circular or spherical may be in error, however. Circles and spheres and waves and ellipses appear Everywhere in nature. But the fundamental dimensions as they are, could be square-like, or cube-like to end the need for the physical gaps, at least, to be filled. Although salts form a cube-like structure, the atoms that comprise the corners of the cube are never, for one, absolutely still, and two, perfectly lin-ear with regards to the edges of the electron clouds being spherical rather than cubed. But the conclusion still leaves us with a logical gap in needing to be resolved (not really, I'm just doing this as my preferred method of meta-negating *Non-Being and Nothingness*), if the Non-Being 0-D point is a cube, from whence cometh circles? For imagination's sake, could the space of 1 Plack length^3 be comprised of a 100-block radius approximate sphere made from Minecraft-like blocks standing in for the cubical Non-Being? Would it be Non-sensical to state the obvious fact that Nothing can be both a sphere and a cube? At the granular scale, a Non-Being is spherical, and at the tiniest of pure dimensional scales, it is cubical, if for no other purpose than to begin making sense of it all again.

In an attempt not to commit philosophical suicide just yet, I shall rephrase this proposition. The dimensions themselves are necessarily transcendental to the thing or things being measured. They never get to the core of describing what the thing(s) actually are, for as I stated earlier, this is-ness of what a thing is requires the totality of its dimensions' values laid out before the thing can be all of what it is. This is impossible, due to its perpetually retroactive nature for those who are Being-in-the-world-alongside-us-in-human-reality. However, this implies that for the objects of appearance to actually be Being-in-the-world-alongside-us-in-human-reality, and not simply Being-a-mere-possibility-as-an-object-of-appearance, all of the dimensions as Being-possible-measure-ments-of-an-object-of-appearance is therefore required before the thing can even begin being what it is, which is its is-ness.

Thus, any philological structure, even one that is based on Nothingness as such, neces-sarily requires at least 1 substantively valid, yet simultaneously transcendental thing from which to compare the soundness of the struc-ture as a means to investigate the thing being measured.

The is-ness of Non-Being and Nothingness is so simple, that it's simple! Do you think that this is complicated? Nah, it's simple, and here is the one sentence that y'all might want to write down in your notes if you're into that sort of thing. *The totality of possible dimensional values for the Non-Being is Non-applicable, and the totality of possible values for every substan-tively valid dimension for Nothingness are all 0.* Just as the empty set's set-ness transcends the emptiness within the set, so do the dimensions transcend the totality of a thing that is Being-measured-in-the-world.

Now, going back to committing philosophical suicide once more, while Nothingness is Being-a-zero-dimensional-cube, comprising the very fabric of the world as a necessary mode of it Being-the-world, the question concerning the number of sides that a 0-D sphere has is clearly Non-applicable. A 0-D cube has both 0 sides & 6 faces, and the question looking into a 0-D sphere's quanta of sides is as inapplicable of an inquiry as it comes, for it would be both 0 and infinite, as is proper for the Non-Being.

Thus, even while the Non-Being is Non-Being, it is Being-a-sphere-of-Non-existence. While it may be alright to visualize a point as a circle or sphere in isolation and a single dimension as a cylinder or string, I hope I have made it clear why when we're constructing an in-total model using valid and substantive dimensions investigating the is-ness of Everything, it would be of benefit to view them as cubical.

Would it be accurate? Who knows besides Nobody? Maybe the gaps between are necessary to hold different kinds of qualia strings for Mass-Electric-Space-Time?

Does it matter? Only a determinist dead-set on actually predicting and explaining Everything should think it does, because that level of precision of empiricism appears to violate Heisenberg's uncertainty principle, and would require, I hypothesize, more energy than what the universe contains to compute, but I digress. There is freedom within the gaps, and I also fear that having the perfect knowledge that would come with genuinely or falsely knowing Everything that will physically happen would not bode well for the human psyche. Catatonia and physical Disequilibrium might even result if the existential anxiety of simply thinking you know what's going to happen next is high enough.

This last chapter may not have been necessary. I intentionally sprinkled stupid words amidst self-proclaimed brilliant ideas in the style of word salads in the realm of pure reason for multiple reasons, and I might as well be clear here about what those intentions were. For one, in the possible future where I am both alive and famous enough to merit attention from this more serious work of mine, I would be able to discern more easily which critiques deserve my time, by whether they chose to criticize an obvious nonsense thing I said, or if they criticize an aspect that I agree needs to be addressed further. Perhaps I could have cut the length of this book in half and still have gotten the points I wanted to across, but it would have been less amusing all-around if I didn't take the sophist liberties that I did. For the witty among you, I hope the nonsense was more of an amusement than a headache. My sincere apologies if that wasn't the case.

And for a genuine personal critique of the pure reason I attempted to address herein, Non-Being cannot be observed, and not being able to observe Nothingness doesn't actually negate the Being of Everything if you cannot have it being-what-Being-is-not. The main point of this book, if one can be made at all, is that Being *likewise* cannot be observed apart from a thing-in-question, and it also adds Nothing to it. So saying that Something is Being, or that Something Exists, is about as useless as saying

Non-Being *is* Nothingness. Only when energy is actualized into action does Being emerge; not before as a part of its is-ness. And energy requires time to demonstrate itself in action, otherwise, it would remain hidden. So before the universe could ever come into Being, if there was a before, what absolutely had to be, was the universe's non-negatable energy in a state of Non-Being. And that is just absurd.